RITES OF PASSAGE

by Ayotunde Oladunjoye also known
as Sonya Mann-McFarlane

RED LEAD PRESS
PITTSBURGH, PENNSYLVANIA 15222

Red Lead Press
701 Smithfield Street
Pittsburgh, PA 15222
Visit our website at www.redleadbooks.com

ISBN: 978-1-4349-6741-1
eISBN: 978-1-4349-2719-4

Acknowledgements

I HAVE RECEIVED A TREMENDOUS AMOUNT OF SUPPORT AND HELP WITH THIS project. First I must thank the Creator, "The Owner, Giver and Taker" of all things. To my Ancestors, known and unknown, thank you for your continued guidance and blessings, as you are greatly loved, honored and appreciated.

To my children, Ayana Imani Mann-Pereira and Chinua Covil-Lette Mann-McFarlane, thank you for your encouragement and involvement to keep this project moving to completion.

Next I owe gratitude to my mentor and advisor, Dr. Michael Penn, as well as countess elders, authors and spiritual guides, which also have inspired me to continue with my work.

To the Imani Edu-Tainers African Dance Company's Board of Directors, my heartfelt thanks for believing in me and the importance of this work.

Many thanks to my friends and colleagues, Jan Bechtel and Samantha Cusacut for their editing and impeccable attention to detail.

Abstract

THE ADOLESCENT PERIOD, BETWEEN CHILDHOOD AND ADULTHOOD, is an important yet prolonged developmental phase. Adolescent pregnancy is a social problem contributing to many challenges associated with this transitional period. Although adolescent pregnancy rates celebrated declines during the 1990's, current rates remain higher among African-American females than Whites. To address this social problem, many African American activists and practitioners have attempted to restore traditional African values, such as explicitly embracing ethnic identity, spirituality and respect for elders and self through the use of rites of passage programs. Adolescent rites of passage intervention strategies are incorporated into youth development programs because of the conviction that mentorship, support and education are necessary if adolescents are to develop into productive, young adults. Such interventions are grounded in the assumption that given appropriate levels of opportunity and attention, adolescents can make significant positive contributions to the communities and societies in which they live.

Introduction

Adolescence is a stage of development marked by the period of time from puberty to the age of maturity (Goggins, 1996). This stage of life, between childhood and adulthood, is an important yet prolonged developmental period during which such profound physical, social and psychological changes occur that many refer to adolescence as a period of transformation. Indeed, with the exception of infancy, there is no other time in the life cycle when transformation and change is so pronounced (Penn & Witkin, 2008).

Adolescent pregnancy is a social problem contributing to the many challenges associated with this transitional period. Although adolescent pregnancy rates in the U.S. celebrated declined during the 1990's, rates remain higher among African-American females than Whites (The Centers for Disease Control and Prevention (CDC), 1997; Adams, 2005). Overall, adolescent pregnancy rates in the U.S. are higher than in any other industrialized country (Ventura, Curtin, Mathews, 1997; Watts Hines, Taylor & Chan, 2007; Santelli, Lindberg, Finer & Singh, 2007).

To address this social problem, African American activists and practitioners have attempted to restore traditional African values, such as an explicit embrace of ethnic identity, spirituality and respect for elders and self through the use of rites of passage programs (Brookins, 1996; Delaney, 1995; Iverem, 1988; Warfield-Copock & Harvey, 1989). Adolescent rites of passage intervention strategies have been incorporated into youth development programs because of the conviction that mentorship, support and education are necessary if adolescents are to develop into productive, young adults. Such interventions are grounded in the assumption that given appropriate levels of opportunity and attention, adolescents can make significant positive contributions to the development of the communities and societies in which they live. Here we examine the nature and philosophical underpinnings of such programs and provide an account for why such programs may be especially helpful in combating high pregnancy rates among African-American adolescents.

Adolescent Pregnancy in the United States

Although American adolescents do not show a significant difference in sexuality patterns when compared to other teens in many industrialized countries, (Coley & Lansdale, 1998) birth rates for females aged 15-19 in European democracies are much lower than those in the United States (The Centers for Disease Control and Prevention (CDC), 1996; 1997). At the beginning of this decade, the rate of adolescent births in the United States was estimated to be twice that of Great Britain (which reports the next highest rate); more than 4 times higher than that of Sweden and Spain; 7 times higher than Denmark and the Netherlands; and 15 times higher than Japan (United Nations, 1991).

One explanation offered for the higher adolescent pregnancy rates in the United States is improper or less frequent use of contraceptives (Santelli, Lindberg, Finer & Singh, 2007; Dixon, Schoonmaker & Philliber, 2000). As compared to their White peers, African-American and Hispanic adolescents are identified as being at higher risk for engaging in sexual intercourse before age 13 and becoming pregnant (Barone, Isokovics, Ayers, Datz, & Voyce 1996; Ventura, Curtin, & Mathews, 1997). In a national school-based study, pregnancy rates of African-American youth were identified at 24 percent, Hispanics at 8.8 percent and Whites at 5.7 percent (CDC, 1995). These data suggest a need for intervention strategies that address the specific needs and circumstances of particular minority populations in the United States.

Hence, adolescent rites of passage intervention strategies are identified as potentially effective in assisting youth to negotiate the many challenges they face while transitioning from childhood into adulthood. For over the last half century, the importance of rites of passage rituals for marking the successful passage from one position in a social structure to another is well documented by anthropologists (Brookins, 1996; Butler & Glennen, 1991; Goggins, 1996; Hill, 1992; Moore, Gilyard, & King, 1987; Warfield-Copock, 1992; Warfield-Coppock & Harvey, 1989).

Furthermore, a rite of passage highlights and legitimizes the move from one social role (that of a child), to a higher level of human social and educational development. This process is facilitated by the community and marks the successful completion of a developmental process that in traditional societies has tended to earn the respect of the community. Rites of passage teach that change is typical and expected, and are timed with common transitional life occurrences. Thus, the primary reason for rites of passage is to orient the participant to the development of inherent qualities and capacities that are not related to status, power and wealth, which will facilitate their overall success in life (O'Neil, 2007; Moore, Gilyard, King, 1987; Brookins, 1996; Delaney; 1995; Iverem, 1988; Warfield-Coppock, 1992; Butler & Glennen, 1991; Mutisya, 1996; Van Gennep, 1960; Onwirah, 1996; Ottenberg, 1992; Warfield-Coppock & Harvey, 1989; Hill, 2002).

Definitions

To aid the reader, the following terms used in this project are defined as: (CDC, 1996; Goggins, 1996)

- **Adolescence**: the developmental stage most often designated as the years from 12-18.
- **Current sexual activity**: sexual intercourse during the three months preceding surveying.
- **Current sexual abstinence**: abstinence during the three months preceding surveying.
- **Preparation**: the stage in which the participant learns what it is to be a rite initiate. The preparation stage starts with recognition of the end in mind.

3

- **Separation**: the stage in which the participant is tested. It is in this stage that the participant must demonstrate the ability to fulfill their responsibilities within the group and their particular stage of life.
- **Transition**: the stage in which the participant is transformed into a rite member. This is usually marked with a ceremony in which the participants enter as an initiate and exit as a member.
- **Rebirth**: the stage in which the new member is presented back to the community. This is also the point at which the new member will be accountable for his or her new responsibilities.

The African-centered Rite of Passage

The African-centered rite of passage process is gender specific and places African traditions at the center of any activity in the rite (Asante, 1987; Brookins, 1996; Delaney, 1995; Warfield-Coppock, 1992; Butler & Glennen, 1991; Mutisya, 1996; Warfield-Coppock & Harvey, 1989; Van Gennep, 1960; Onwirah, 1996; Ottenberg, 1992; Goggins, 1996; Hill, 1992). Accordingly, specific terms are important in articulating an African-centered rites of passage perspective (Goggins, 1996). For example, "adolescence" is the developmental stage most often designated as the years from 12-18. "Preparation" consists of the stage in which the participant learns the requirements of being a rite initiate and begins with recognition of the end that is to be achieved; "separation" refers to the stage in which the participant is tested, hence the stage that the participant must demonstrate the ability to fulfill the responsibilities within the group that are appropriate for the particular stage of life that they are about to enter; "transition" is the stage in which the participant is transformed into a rite member, usually marked by a ceremony in which the participants enter as an initiate and exit as members and "rebirth" refers to the stage during which the new member is presented back to the community, and thus the point at which the new member will be accountable for his or her new responsibilities.

In this context, the basic elements of a rite of passage include: separation from society, preparation and instruction from an elder, a transition (for example, from adolescent to adult), and a rebirth or welcoming back into society with emphasis placed on the individual's changed status. The ceremonies that accompany various stages of a rite generally include: cleansing (literal and spiritual), a symbolic physical transformation, offerings, prayers and blessings, traditional food and dress, and use of traditional musical instruments, dance and song (Brookins, 1996; Delaney, 1995; Warfield-Coppock, 1992; Butler & Glennen, 1991; Mutisya, 1996; Warfield-Coppock & Harvey, 1989; Van Gennep, 1960; Onwirah, 1996; Ottenberg, 1992; Goggins, 1996; Hill, 1992).

4

Thus, rites of passage programs aim to achieve one or more objectives which include activities to promote bonding, foster resilience, promote social, emotional, cognitive, behavioral and moral competence, foster self-determination, spirituality, self-efficacy, clear and positive identity, promote belief in the future, provide recognition for positive behavior and opportunities for pro-social involvement, and foster self-determination (Catalano, Berglund, Ryan, Lonczak, & Hawkins, 2002).

Prior to the on-set of the mid-Atlantic slave trade industry and colonization, rites of passage rituals were a part of the socialization process for regenerating West African and Central African communities (Hill, 2002). However, the importance of rites of passage rituals for marking the successful passage from one position in a social structure to another has been documented by anthropologists (Moore, Gilyard, King, 1987; Brookins, 1996; Delaney; 1995; Iverem, 1988; Warfield-Coppock; 1992; Butler & Glennen, 1991; Mutisya, 1996; Van Gennep, 1960; Onwirah, 1996; Ottenberg, 1992; Warfield-Coppock & Harvey, 1989).

During the past two decades, there has been an increase in interest in rites of passage. The surge in interest is attributed to the rise in African-centered consciousness through research, writing and teaching of African-centered scholars over the past three decades (Hill, 2002; Potts, 2003; Madhubuti & Madhubuti, 1994). Several studies support the general proposition that knowledge and respect for African culture may be positively linked with improved health and academic outcomes for youth of African descent (Potts, 2003).

For example, the use of African-centered rituals in advancing positive youth development, and their value in developing a healthy cultural consciousness has been confirmed in a study of the Benjamin E. Mays Institute (BEMI) in Hartford, Connecticut, where rite of passage training is a major program component and approach to education (Potts, 2003). BEMI functions from an African-centered prospective within a middle school serving a community of people of African descent in Hartford, Connecticut. BEMI students outperform other students academically. Additionally, using the Racial Identity Attitude Scale and the Multi-group Ethnic Identity Measure to compare all middle school students at the same school, results showed higher scores in racial and ethnic identity among students enrolled at BEMI (Potts, 2003). Higher levels of ethnic identity have been related to less risky sexual attitudes among African-American adolescent females (Belgrave, Van Oss Marin, & Chambers, 2000). This research supports the view that knowledge of African culture, a foundation of rite of passage training, may be positively associated with improved health outcomes and academic success for adolescents of African descent.

Pregnancy Prevention Interventions

Intervention programs aimed at reducing teenage pregnancy have employed several strategies to provide knowledge of sexual reproduction and contraceptives and given adolescents access to contraceptives; they have reinforced values; taught abstinence; built decision-making and social skills; and increased awareness of life options (Frost & Forrest, 1995; Kirby, 1997; Maynard, 1997; Miller, Card, Paikoff & Peterson, 1992; Miller & Paikoff, 1992). Programs producing successful results in delaying sexual activity among adolescents tend to teach abstinence and provide information and access to contraceptive for older teens (Frost & Forrest, 1995). Three programs using African-centered interventions with demonstrated effectiveness in delaying the initiation of sexual intercourse or increasing contraceptive use among those having intercourse, are noted here.

1. Be Proud! Be Responsible (Jemmott & Jemmott, 1992)
2. Becoming a Responsible Teen (St. Lawrence; Brasfield, Jefferson, Alleyne, O'Bannon, 1995)
3. Focus on Kids (Galbraith, Ricardo, Stanton, Black, Feigelman, Kaljee, 1996)

The Children's Aid Society's Teen Pregnancy Prevention Program and "I Have A Future," initiated by Meharry Medical College implemented some common intervention strategies like those suggested in rite of passage programming (Foster, Greene, & Smith, 1990). Both community-based programs addressed the problem of adolescent pregnancy and targeted at-risk youth as young as 10 years of age. Family members were also involved in the training and education. These programs promoted improved self-esteem, sexual responsibility, responsible citizenship, physical and mental well-being, school completion and development and enhancement of job skills. Evaluated indicators of The Children's Aid Society's program demonstrated the following (1994):

1. School retention: 90 percent retention rate for The Children's Aid Society, compared to a 50 percent retention rate for non-participants enrolled in city school districts.
2. Pregnancy: during the first four years, in which more than 800 youth were served, only eight were known to become pregnant.
3. Education: 75 percent of Children's Aid Society students were admitted to college in 1994.

Extreme difficulty was reported with identifying and evaluating many adolescent prevention programs that have documented significant success. The reason for this was that only a few programs addressed the risk factors consistently found to predict adolescent pregnancy in research studies. Such factors include poverty, early school failure, early behavioral problems, and family problems or dysfunction. For programs that did focus on these risk factors, few started at an early age or targeted several risk factors simultaneously. Programs reviewed tended to have a narrow focus on a single aspect of prevention, were brief, and were provided too late in life to have a major impact among at-risk populations (Moore, Miller, Glei, and Morrison, 1995). Abstinence-only programs focus on the importance of abstaining from sexual intercourse until marriage. Six published studies of abstinence-only programs found that program completion had no significant effect on delaying intercourse (cited in Kirby, 1997).

A review was conducted of evaluation literature from 55 adolescent pregnancy prevention curricula. Materials to assist with the evaluation of these curricula were made available through the Program Archive on Sexuality, Health, and Adolescence (Card, Niego, Mallari and Farrell, 1996). The evaluation results of reviewed curricula had to meet two criteria: (1) if the program had been designed for teens at least 16 years of age, the program must have produced a positive impact upon sexual or contraceptive behavior of one or more subgroups of youth; and (2) if the program was designed for youth under 16 years of age, the program must have produced an effect upon relevant attitudes, skills, intentions or values. These curricula were rated on a scale of 1-10. Of the 55 curricula selected for review, 30 were found with mean scores of 6.5 or higher, and as having significant effect on adolescent pregnancy prevention. Nearly all the prevention interventions incorporated behavioral skills development (e.g. negotiating condom use, practicing saying no and practicing how to avoid risky situations), contraceptive education and sexuality education into their approach. A review of published literature including on-going reviews conducted by The Division of Adolescent and School Health within the Federal Centers for Disease Control and Prevention, identified four curricula as having demonstrated evidence for changing risky sexual behaviors (Kirby, 1997).

1. Becoming a Responsible Teen
2. Be Proud! Be Responsible!
3. Get Real about AIDS
4. Reducing the Risk

No single solution or intervention was seen to be effective over and above the others, suggesting that adolescent pregnancy rates would be best impacted by multiple interventions. The goal of reaching a broad teen audience and the implementation of a combination of strategies that involve key members of the community was suggested (Herdman; 1996; Philliber

& Namerow, 1995; Kirby, 1997; Moore & Sugland, 1996; Moore, Miller, Glei, & Morrison, 1995; Davis, 1996).

Comprehensive evaluations of adolescent pregnancy prevention programs are described as a critical component in understanding the complexities of teen pregnancies (Moore & Sugland, 1996; Catalano, et al., 2002). Barriers to implementation including cost, limited time and resources and small sample size have complicated the evaluation process of many prevention programs (Moore, 1996; Moore & Sugland, 1996; Herdman, 1996; Philliber & Namerow, 1995; Catalano, et al., 2002).

This research suggests that an effective African-centered approach to reducing pregnancy rates among African-American adolescents, and adolescents of African descent, must not only include learning activities and experiences targeting increased knowledge of African culture, but should also address more than one risk factor consistently found to predict adolescent pregnancy. Additionally, an effective Afrocentric approach to adolescent pregnancy prevention can employ abstinence as a pregnancy prevention strategy, but should not be used as a "stand-alone" intervention strategy.

A Traditional Rite of Passage

An African-centered (or traditional) rite of passage is gender specific, and places African traditions at the center of any activity or idea included in the rite (Asante, 1987; Brookins, 1996; Delaney, 1995; Warfield-Coppock, 1992; Butler & Glennen, 1991; Mutisya, 1996; Warfield-Coppock & Harvey, 1989; Van Gennep, 1960; Onwirah, 1996; Ottenberg, 1992; Goggins, 1996; Hill, 1992). The basic elements of a rite of passage are:

1. Separation from society.
2. Preparation and instruction from an elder.
3. A transition (for example, from adolescent to adult).
4. Rebirth or welcoming back into society with emphasis placed on the individual's changed status.

The ceremonies that are done at various stages of a rite generally include:

1. Cleansing - literal and spiritual.
2. Physical transformation.
3. Offerings, prayers and blessings.
4. Traditional food and dress.
5. Traditional musical instruments, dance and songs (Brookins, 1996; Delaney, 1995; Warfield-Coppock, 1992; Butler & Glennen, 1991; Mutisya, 1996; Warfield-Coppock & Harvey, 1989; Van Gennep,

1960; Onwirah, 1996; Ottenberg, 1992; Goggins, 1996; Hill, 1992).

Positive communication between parent and child was found to be a vital element in a traditional rite of passage (Warfield-Coppock, 1992; Goggins, 1996; Warfield-Coppock & Harvey, 1989). Parent-child communication was also found to be an important ingredient in the growth of adolescents, whose values, goals, self-esteem and decision-making skills promote good health (Phinney & Chavira, 1995; Flannery, Torquanti, Lindemeier, 1994).

Commonalities among Principles of Interventions and Prevention Programs

Commonalities among principles of prevention programs and interventions reviewed here provide guidelines and a rationale for the implementation of rite of passage training programs designed to prevent pregnancies among African-American adolescents, and adolescents of African descent. These common principles address topics ranging from the focus of intervention efforts to target populations and the characteristics of programs, to the need for evaluation. The principles include:

1. Structure the intervention based on the findings of basic research and previous program evaluation studies.
2. Begin interventions for at-risk youth before the onset of puberty.
3. Include family and community in programming.
4. Create activities that are appropriate for the age and developmental stage of participants.
5. Set defined and realistic program goals.
6. Provide culturally appropriate program activities.
7. Coordinate message to specifically target males and females.
8. Provide information on both abstinence and contraception, and ensure access to contraceptive services.
9. Conduct process evaluations, and as required, conduct rigorous impact evaluations (Moore & Sugland, 1996; Davis, 1996; Philliber & Namerow, 1995; Catalano, et al., 2002; Madhubuti & Madhubuti, 1994; Dixon; Schoonmaker & Philliber, 2000).

In addition to the guiding principles listed above, the following recommendations are encouraged when considering the implementation of a rite of passage training program:

1. The program should be evaluated and updated annually by parents, program graduates and community members.
2. The status of program graduates should be tracked, evaluated and documented annually through college or post high school training.

9

3. The program should expand services and educational activities to accommodate the changing needs of program participants.

Therefore, in considering the implementation of a rite of passage training program, the program should be evaluated and updated at least annually, and the status of the program graduates should be tracked, evaluated and documented. Ongoing comprehensive evaluations of rite of passage training programs that target pregnancy prevention will provide valid recommendations for ongoing program enhancements that will assist practitioners with adopting services and educational activities to accommodate the changing needs of the program participants.

A rite of passage is a permission to move from one level in society to a higher level of human social and educational development. This permission is granted by the community and marks the successful completion of a developmental process and the earning of the respect of the community (Moore, Gilyard & King, 1987; Brookins, 1996; Delaney, 1995; Iverem, 1988; Warfield-Coppock, 1992; Butler & Glennen, 1991; Mutisya, 1996; Van Gennep, 1960; Onwirah, 1996; Ottenberg, 1992; Warfield-Coppock & Harvey, 1989). African-Americans have attempted to restore traditional African values such as ethnic identity, spirituality and respect for elders, self and community, through the use of traditional and non-traditional rites of passage programs (Brookins; Delaney, 1995; Iverem, 1988; Warfield-Copock, 1992).

Rite of passage training programs that include pregnancy prevention intervention strategies, have been proven effective in assisting adolescents with the transition into young adulthood. Pregnancy continues to be one of the social problems confronting adolescents, challenging their successful transition. Adolescent pregnancy has a negative impact on individuals, families, communities and society. Adolescent parents face tremendous hardships and place a significant financial burden on society. Considering African-American and Hispanic youth have been identified as being at higher risk for having sexual intercourse before age 13 and becoming pregnant than Whites in a national school-based study; 24, 8.8, and 5.7 percent respectively, an African-centered rite of passage intervention, targeting adolescent pregnancy prevention, should include strategies proven effective in:

1. Assisting adolescents with transitioning into young adulthood.
2. Improving health outcomes.
3. Assisting families and communities with restoring traditional African values such as ethnic identity, spirituality and respect for

elders and self (CDC, 1995; Barone, Isokovics, Ayers, Datz, & Voyce, 1996).

Through the successful completion of rite of passage training, participants gain a sense of increased self-esteem, self-image and awareness, as well as enhanced skills required for responsible sexual decision-making and goal setting. These strategies have been proven effective toward pregnancy prevention among adolescents.

It is suggested that a rite of passage, which serves to mark a time when a person reaches a new and significant change in his/her life, is something that nearly all societies recognize. Rite of passage ceremonies hold an immense value as they observe and celebrate a person's entry into a new stage of life. Through a continued interest in African-centered rites of passage training programs, families and communities are reminded of the importance of their collective efforts united for the common good of raising children, thus further emphasizing successful transition for adolescents into young adulthood. These strategies have been proven to be effective toward pregnancy prevention among adolescents, which remains one of our most destructive social problems. Thus, they deserve further attention from researchers and practitioners.

MATE MASIE - "WHAT I HEAR, I KEEP" RITE OF PASSAGE TRAINING PROGRAM

IN LANCASTER, PENNSYLVANIA, THE RATE OF TEEN PREGNANCY AMONG INNER-CITY minorities was found to be higher than the national average (Lancaster County Health Partnership, 1997; Community Needs Report, 1995). The birth rate for adolescents ages 15-19 declined by one during 1995 and 1996, and the 1997 Census estimated the population rate among these groups to have grown several times higher than the total population in Lancaster County (Pennsylvania Department of Health, 1995 & 1996, Delaney, 1998).

Akuaba, a rite of passage curriculum, was developed to address adolescent pregnancy prevention (Mann-McFarlane, 1998). Mate Masie - "What I Hear, I Keep", is a rite of passage training program, adopted by the Imani Edu-Tainers African Dance Company that incorporates the Akuaba curriculum. This training program targets African-American females and females of African descent ages 12-21 in Lancaster, Pennsylvania, and combines traditional rite of passage practices with proven intervention strategies, effective in adolescent pregnancy, and successful transition into young adulthood.

Traditional rituals and ceremonies related to traditional rites of passage are incorporated into this program. The concept of separation from the community as a child and returning (rebirth) as a responsible adult is key. While separated from immediate family members, participants receive intense instruction from elders of the community and participate in ritual bathing. Ritual bathing symbolizes casting off the old. These activities are conducted within a nature-friendly environment, free from societal distraction including television, telephone and electronic devices. The periods of separation also serve to foster closer bonding of the participants.

12

Celebrating the completion of a rite of passage is extremely important to the participants and to the community to which they are returning. The transformation from childhood into young adulthood is highlighted, and the celebration observes African customs and rituals (food music, dance, traditional dress, libation and prayer), including the young ladies who participated at all levels of program implementation and delivery. This is also the time when the community will be informed of participants' successful completion.

Mate Masie combines traditional rites of passage practices with proven intervention strategies effective in adolescent pregnancy prevention, to assist adolescents with the transition into young adulthood. This program's educational training period consists of eight lesson plans developed to explore each topical area in detail. Each lesson plan contains learning goals, objectives, content and resources. A parent orientation is included with the educational training sessions, with initial program entry. When comparing Mate Masie program participants to non-participants, results show that the program had a positive impact on reducing the incidence of teen pregnancy. Mate Masie targets African-American female adolescents, and its program components focus on:

1. Self identity
2. Ancestral and family history
3. Healthy attitudes
4. Decision-making
5. Sexuality education
6. Goal-setting
7. Reducing sexual risk
8. West African dance and rhythms

This multi-year program recruits participants while in middle school and their ongoing participation is encouraged through college. Program success is highlighted at a graduation ceremony, with family and friends in attendance. During the program, participants reflect on the importance of the four program components through personal presentations. Participants who successfully complete the programs meet monthly to reinforce the importance of self-knowledge, self-development and self-esteem.

Mate Masie – "What I Hear, I Keep"
Educational Activity Guide

The primary goal of this program is to combine traditional rite of passage practices with proven intervention strategies effective in adolescent pregnancy prevention, to assist adolescents with the transition into young adulthood. In order to achieve this goal, a parent orientation is included with eight topical areas for the program educational training period. The topical areas developed are:

- Self identity
- Ancestral and family history
- Healthy attitudes
- Decision-making
- Sexuality education
- Goal-setting
- Reducing sexual risk
- African dance and rhythms

The educational training session consists of eight lesson plans developed to explore each topical area in detail. Each lesson plan contains learning goals, objectives, content and resources. The lessons vary in length and are to be implemented as part of the rite of passage training period. In addition to the educational training sessions, traditional rituals and ceremonies related to traditional rites of passage will be incorporated into this program.

Separation and Preparation

The concept of separation from the community as a child and returning (rebirth) as a responsible young adult is key to traditional rites of passage. As part of this program, separation from immediate family members is enforced. The amount of time for separation periods varies. Participants receive intense instruction from elders of the community and participate in ritual bathing. Ritual bathing symbolizes casting off the old, and will initially be done by an African religious leader. The last ritual bath symbolizes rebirth and will be performed by the participants' mothers on the morning of the "welcoming back to the community" celebration.

Transition and Rebirth

At the decision of the elder conducting the rite of passage program, transition is announced. This time marks the end of the seclusion and training period. This is usually marked with a ceremony in which the participant enters as an initiate and exits as a member. Rebirth is the stage in

14

which the new member is presented back to the community. This is also the point at which the new member will be accountable for his or her new responsibilities.

Celebrating the completion of a rite of passage is extremely important to the participants and to the community to which they are returning. This is the time when the community will be informed of the successful completion of the tasks and activities assigned during the training period. The transformation from childhood into young adulthood is highlighted at the celebration. African customs and rituals (food music, dance, traditional dress, libation and prayer) are observed at the celebration.

These training activities are conducted within a friendly environment, free from societal distraction including television, telephone, popular music and video games. The periods of separation will also serve to foster closer bonding of the participants.

Parent Orientation

Goal: To increase parental knowledge of traditional rites of passage practices using oral, written and visual materials.

Objective: Upon completion, the parents will be able to describe the four stages that will be incorporated into this rite of passage program.

Methods:

1. Review program brochure.
2. Question and Answer:
    a. What is traditional rite of passage?
        i. Discuss parent responses.
3. Why is it important to implement this rite of passage?
        i. Discuss and record parent responses.
4. View the video "Monday's Girl".
    a. Identify and discuss the rite of passage stages and ceremonies presented in the video.
5. Distribute bibliography and notes on rite of passage literature.
    a. Discuss similarities reviewed in the literature and this rite of passage program

Goal: To increase parent's knowledge of the components of this traditional rite of passage program, using oral and written materials.

Objectives: The parents will be able to:

1. List the eight educational sessions covered in this rite of passage program.
2. Describe the ceremonies and rituals that will be incorporated into this program

Methods:

1. Review and discuss program activities.

Goal: To increase parent's awareness of the importance of parent-child communication in adolescent pregnancy prevention.

Objective: The parents will:

1. A. Discuss the importance of positive parent-child communication in preventing adolescent pregnancy.

Methods:

1. Review and discuss Ten tips for parents to help their children avoid teen pregnancy.
2. Review and discuss Parent-child communication: Promoting healthy youth.

Goal: Increase parents' awareness of the local problem of adolescent pregnancy and its impact on family, community and society.

Objectives: Parents will:

1. Become familiar with the regional and local statistics on adolescent pregnancy.
2. Discuss how an adolescent pregnancy within their own family would impact their lives.

Methods:

1. Literature review:
2. Discuss the local statistics related to adolescent pregnancy.
3. Discussion:
   a. Verbalize how adolescent pregnancies within the community affect their lives.
   b. Verbalize how an adolescent pregnancy occurring with their child would affect their family.

Resources:

Advocates For Youth. (2009) Parent-child communication: Promoting healthy youth. Washington, DC: Author.

Advocates For Youth. (2002) Adolescent sexual behavior: Demographics. Washington, DC: Author.

Onwirah, N. (1996). Monday's Girl. The Library of African Cinema. Penn State University.

The National Campaign to Prevent Teen and Unplanned Pregnancy. (2007) Ten tips for parents to help their children avoid teen pregnancy. Washington, DC: Author.

Ten Tips for Parents to Help Their Children Avoid Teen Pregnancy

The National Campaign to Prevent Teen Pregnancy has reviewed recent research about parental influences on children's sexual behavior and talked to many experts in the field, as well as to teens and parents themselves. From these sources, it is clear that parents and adults can be instrumental in reducing the risk of adolescents becoming sexually active and becoming pregnant.

1. **Be clear about your own sexual values and attitudes. To clarify your attitudes and values think about the following kinds of questions:**
   a. What do you really think about school-aged teenagers being sexually active?
   b. Who is responsible for setting sexual limits in a relationship and how is that done, realistically?
   c. What do you think about encouraging adolescents to abstain from sex?
   d. What do you think about adolescents (ages 12-14) using contraceptives?
2. **Talk to your children early and often about sex, and be specific.**
3. **Supervise and monitor your children and adolescents.**
4. **Know your child's friends and their families.**
5. **Discourage early, frequent and steady dating.**
6. **Take a strong stand against your daughter dating a boy significantly older than her.**
7. **Help your adolescent have options for the future that are more attractive than early pregnancy and parenthood.**
8. **Let your children know that you value education.**
9. **Know what your children are reading, watching and listening to.**
10. **The first nine steps work best when they occur as part of a strong, close relationship, with your child that is built from an early age.**

Adapted from: The National Campaign To Prevent Teen Pregnancy. (2007).

The Facts About Parent-Child Communication

Positive communication between parent and child is a vital element in the growth of adolescents into confident young adults whose values, goals, self-esteem and decision-making skills will promote emotional and physical health.

IT'S A FACT

Parent-child communication promotes health, achievement and self-esteem.

Good relationships between adolescents and parents are consistently associated with positive and healthy self-esteem. African-American teens whose parents have discussed both achievement and disproving strategies to counter stereotypes and racism demonstrate higher self-esteem than teens whose parents ignore social issues.

Lack of communication affects behaviors and attitudes.

Adolescents who perceive little support from their parents also report more school problems, drug and alcohol use, delinquent acts and serious crime than adolescents who perceive strong parental support. Studies showed that seventh and eight grade students correctly estimated how upset their parents would be at learning their child was using drugs, but significantly underestimated how upset they would be to discover their child was having sex.

Talking about sex and values fosters better health.

A study of African-American adolescents found that simply perceived maternal strictness was related to decreased sexual intercourse and fewer sexual partners and parental strictness was related to fewer sexual partners and increased condom usage. Adolescents who reported previous discussion of sexual matters with parents were seven and a half times more likely to feel able to communicate with a partner about AIDS than those who had not had such discussions.

Adapted from: Advocates for Youth. (2009). Parent-child communications: Promoting healthy youth.

Participant Orientation

Goal: To increase participants' knowledge of traditional rites of passage practices using oral, written and visual materials.

Objectives: The participants will be able to:
1. Describe the four stages that will be incorporated into this rites of
2. passage program.
3. Describe the rituals and ceremonies that will be incorporated into this
4. rite of passage program.

Methods:
1. Question and Answer:
   a. What is a traditional rite of passage?
   b. Discuss responses.
   c. What is an adolescent rite of passage?
2. Why is it important to you to participate in this program?
   a. Discuss and list responses.
   b. View the video "Monday's Girl".
   c. Identify and discuss the rite of passage stages and ceremonies presented in the video.

Goal: To provide a safe and respectful environment conducive for open group discussions.

Objectives: Participants will understand the characteristics of acceptable program behavior
1. Review and explain the characteristics of acceptable program behavior:
2. Introduce the program's Conduct Contract.
3. Discuss the Conduct Contract.
4. Identify posted rules of conduct.
5. Sign Conduct Contracts to reinforce conduct rules.
6. Have participants obtain parent's signature on Conduct Contracts and return.

Methods:
1. Post and distribute conduct rules.
2. Discuss conduct rules.
3. Obtain two signed copies (parents' and participants') of signed Conduct Contact.

Adapted from:Guide *to* Implementing TAP: A Peer Education Program to Prevent HIV and STI (2nd edition), © 2002, Advocates for Youth, Washington, DC

Conduct Contract

This Conduct Contract has been developed to establish a comfortable environment, conducive for open group discussion and sharing. It is important that we all understand and follow the rules of this contract. Please read carefully and thoroughly. Ask any questions you may have before signing.

Conduct Rules

- ✓ All information shared with the group will remain **confidential.**
- ✓ Be **open and honest**.
- ✓ Never use someone else's name in a group discussion that is not present. Use examples and general statements but not identifying descriptions.
- ✓ **Do not judge** or put down someone else.
- ✓ It is **OK** to disagree.
- ✓ **Participate.** Use your right to *pass* thoughtfully.
- ✓ There **are no dumb questions**. Use the *Question Box* for anonymous questions.
- ✓ Use "I" statements as opposed to "you".
- ✓ Have FUN.

Parent Signature _____

Participant Signature _____

Adapted from:Guide to Implementing TAP: A Peer Education Program to Prevent HIV and STI (2nd edition), © 2002, Advocates for Youth, Washington, DC

Session One

Self Identity

Goal: To introduce the term "adolescence."
Objectives: Upon completion, participants will be able to:
1. Define adolescence.
2. Communicate with parents or other adult family members about their perception and experiences of being an adolescent.

Methods: Lecture/Group discussion.
1. Ask group to define adolescence.
2. Explain to the group that becoming an adolescent does not make you a new person, but it does make you a person who is or will be going through a great deal of change - physical, emotional, and mental.
3. Ask the participants to describe what adolescence is or has been like. Record key responses.
4. Ask participants to explain why they think adolescence is both exciting and challenging. Record key responses.
5. Distribute "Adult Interview" homework. Ask participants to discuss the questions on the handout with their parents or another adult family member.

Note: Emphasize to the group that this should be an enjoyable activity for them and the interviewee. They should take their time to listen to the interviewee and record responses accurately.

Goals:
1. Increase participants' awareness of how symbols are used to portray self-identity and group characteristics.
2. Increase participants' knowledge of Adinkra art symbols and their use in portraying self and group characteristics.

Objectives: Upon completion, participants will be able to:
1. Recognize several Adinkra art symbols and their meaning.
2. Associate an Adinkra art symbol with a personal characteristic.
3. Create a personal design using a minimum of three Adinkra symbols.

Methods: Use of Adinkra Symbolism to identify personal traits and characteristics
1. Distribute handouts on Adinkra Symbolism and current teen magazines.

22

2. Question and answer:
   a. What is Adinkra art?
   b. Discuss and record responses.
3. Why is symbolism important?
4. Distribute copies of questions "Who am I"?
5. Create a design using a minimum of three Adinkra symbols, and other magazine pictures that answers the questions on the "Who am I?" handout.
6. Group presentations and discussion of designs.

Resources:

Hunter-Geboy, Carol. Life Planning Education: A Youth Development Program. Washington, DC: Advocates for Youth, 1995.

Well Tempered Web Designs (2007). West African Wisdom: Adinkra Symbols & Meanings. http://adinkra.org/

Kojo, G. (1998). Akan Cultural Symbols Project. http://marshall.edu/akanartintro.html

Ansa K. (1993). Adinkrah Symbols. http://auvsi.org/kemet/adinkra.htm.

Who Am I?

1. What or who do you value most in your life?

2. What are five things you do well?

3. What would you like most to be remembered for?

4. What is one important thing you have done in life?

5. What do your friends really like about you?

6. Choose three positive adjectives that best describe your best qualities.

Adult Interview

Name_____Relationship_____

Interview a parent or another adult in your family about his or her adolescence. Here are some questions to ask.

1. What was adolescent life like for you?
2. What were your most embarrassing moments?
3. What were your long-term goals?
4. What kind of disagreements did you have with your parents?
5. Do you feel that young people mature earlier today than they did three generations ago?

Source: Core-Gebhart, P., Hart, S., & Young, M. (1994) Sex Can Wait. ETR Associates: Santa Cruz, CA

Session Two

Ancestral and Family History

Goal: To increase skills in research and writing reports.

Objective: Participants will complete a research project to include a minimum of four references.

Methods: View the television series "Africans in America". (This activity will take place over the course of this program. A major part of the program viewing will be done during the separation component of the program)

1. Visit to computer lab/library.
2. Research sources to support at least three components reviewed in Africans in America.
3. Completed Research project of a one-page summary of each program component of "Africans in America."

Goals:

1. Increase participants' knowledge of their living and ancestral family members.
2. Involve parents in constructing the family tree.

Objective: Design/construct a family tree of at least four generations...

Methods:

1. Collect data from family members including names, dates, birthplaces, etc.
2. Identify family historian.
3. Provide photographs if possible.
4. Provide a lecture focusing on genealogy research and the construction of a "Family Tree". A professional(s) in the field will facilitate this activity.
5. Distribute model of family tree.
6. Distribute handouts on Adinkra history and art symbols.
7. Design a draft of the family tree on paper, and return draft with parents' signature to validate accuracy. Use the input of parents to apply Adinkra art symbols that best describes or symbolizes their closest ancestor.

Note: Time will be allotted for work on the family tree project throughout the program. Participants will present their completed projects to their parents at the *Celebration Ceremony*.

Resources:

Africans in America TV Series & Beyond. http://www.pbs.org

Black Americans of Achievement. (1993). BAOA, Inc., San Diego, CA.

Kojo, G. (1998). Akan Cultural Symbols Project. http://marshall.edu/akanartintro. html

Ansa K. (1993). Adinkrah Symbols. http://auvsi.org/kemet/adinkra.htm

Heinegg, P. (1997). Free African Americans of North Carolina and Virginia. Baltimore, MD: The Genealogical Publishing Company.

The Afrigeneas Homepage. (1998). http://www.msstate. edu/Archives/History/ afrigen/

Kepple, D. (1998). Tracing Your History. Dayton Daily News. Dayton, Ohio. http://members.aol.com.gfsclint/bennie1.html

The African Ancestored Database. (1997). http://members. aol.com.afriamgene/ surnames/sig-names.html

Session Three

Healthy Attitudes

Goal: Increase participant's knowledge about the benefits of a positive attitude.

Objectives: Upon completion, participants will have a better understanding of:

1. How positive attitudes help us feel good about ourselves.
2. How positive attitudes help us relate well with others.
3. How positive attitudes help us have a vision of personal future goals.

Methods: Lecture/Group discussion

Introduction: Our attitudes influence how we think, feel and act. The benefits of positive attitudes include:

- ✓ Helping us feel good about ourselves.
- ✓ Helping us relate well with others.
- ✓ **Helping us to have a vision of personal future goals.**
- ✓ **Our attitudes can also be called our "mental sets".**

1. Distribute handout "Ten Mental Sets". Explain to the group that these mental sets can help develop and maintain positive attitudes about themselves and others.
2. Discuss the mental sets. Allow the participants the opportunity to reword, but not change the concept, to fit their talking and communication styles.
3. Hand out index cards. Tell participant to choose up to three mental sets they think would be useful for them to work on. Emphasize that over time and with practice these sets will become an integral part of their view of life. Encourage the participants to refer to these mental sets in the future to continue positive attitudes enhancement.

Food for Thought: A positive attitude is powerful. You must first believe in yourself before you expect that from others.

Ten Mental Sets

These ten mental sets are statements that will help you maintain a positive attitude and healthy self-esteem. Our attitudes influence how we think, feel and act. Practice the ones that are meaningful to you. You can gradually make them part of our life.

Note: Don't make these affirmations into "shoulds" for yourself. Be gentle with yourself as you practice them. You should see results when you introduce these attitudes into your daily life.

1. I do the best I can about a situation. I try to resolve it without worrying.
2. I set realistic goals for myself. I do one thing at a time.
3. I am aware of my own feelings, and can choose to express them honestly to other people. I am responsible "to" other people, not responsible "for" them.
4. I choose how to respond to situations and accept responsibility for my choices.
5. I have no need to compare myself to other people or to compete with them.
6. I treat all others with the respect and acceptance I wish for myself.
7. I realize there are options in any situation and feel the freedom to explore them.
8. I learn lessons and grow from both positive and negative experiences.
9. I think and live positively, committing myself to achieving personal excellence. If I backside, I can stop and get back on track.
10. I live in the present moment, but I realize I can learn from the past and I have hope for the future.

Adapted from: Core-Gebhart, P., Hart, S., & Young, M. (1994) Sex Can Wait. ETR Associates: Santa Cruz, CA

Introduction to Sexuality

Goal: To introduce the concept of sexuality.
Objective: To develop a broad definition of sexuality
Methods:

1. Distribute and display the five concepts of sexuality. Explain that everything related to sexuality fits into the five concepts that make up the different components of sexuality.
2. Review and discuss components of sexuality:
   a. **Sensuality** - the awareness, acceptance of and comfort with your body; psychological and physiological enjoyment of your body and the body of others.
   b. **Sexualization** - the use of sexuality to control others.
   c. **Intimacy** - emotional closeness to another person.
   d. **Sexual health and reproduction** - attitudes and behaviors related to producing children, care of sex and reproductive organs, and health consequences of sexual behavior.
   e. **Sexual identity** - the developed sense of who you are sexually, including sense of maleness and femaleness.
3. Encourage group discussion by asking for examples of behaviors that would relate to the concepts.

Discussion points

1. Which of the five concepts feels most familiar? Why?
2. Is there any part of these concepts that you never thought of as being "sexual" before?
3. Which concept is most important for people your age to know about? Least important?
4. Which concept would you be interested in discussing with your parent(s)?
5. Which concept would you be interested in talking about with someone you were dating?

Goal: To define sexuality in a more concrete way through the use of visual images and written materials.
Objective: Upon completion, participants will develop images of what the term sexuality means to them.
Methods:

1. Display sexuality concepts and briefly mention previous discussion that broadly defined sexuality.

2. Instruct participants to construct a collage using current magazines, pictures, songs and lyrics to illustrate a concept discussed previously.
3. Ask each participant to display and present their collage, explaining the images they chose for their concept.

Discussion points:
1. Is anything missing from your concept collage that should be added? What and why?
2. What were the most difficult aspects of your sexuality concept to depict with the available images?
3. Which concept of sexuality would be the hardest to explain to a parent or a younger sibling? Why?

Goal: To reinforce accurate information related to sexuality and reproduction.

Objective:
1. Assess participants' awareness of facts related to sexuality and reproduction by:
2. Participating in a "Fact or Fiction" Bowl.
3. Participating in-group discussion of responses to questions used in the bowl.

Methods: Group competition in quiz activity and discussion.
1. Divide the group into two teams and have them compete against each other. Award a point to each team for each correct answer.

Fact or Fiction Bowl

1. Once a girl has had her first period, she can become pregnant.
2. Most adolescents have had sexual intercourse by the time they finish high school.
3. A girl can become pregnant before she has her first period.
4. Abstinence is the only method of contraception that is 100 % effective.
5. Douching will prevent pregnancy.
6. A girl has to be 18 years old to get contraception from a clinic without a parent's consent.
7. Adolescents can be treated for STD's without their parents' permission.
8. Males need to have sex to keep good health.
9. There is no cure for herpes.
10. A woman cannot get pregnant if she has sexual intercourse during her period.
11. It is unhealthy for a girl to bathe (bathtub) or swim during her period.
12. Condoms are not very effective in preventing pregnancy or STD's
13. Only females can have sexually transmitted diseases without symptoms.
14. A woman can always calculate the "safe" time during her menstrual cycle when she can have vaginal intercourse and be protected from pregnancy.
15. Once a person has had gonorrhea and been cured, he/she cannot get it again.

Discussion points:

1. What fact surprised you the most?
2. Are there other myths or fictional concepts related to sexuality and reproduction you can think of and would be willing to share with the group?

Adapted from:Life Planning Education. (1995). Advocates for Youth. Washington, DC

Concepts of Sexuality

- *Sensuality*- Awareness, acceptance of and comfort with your body. Psychological and physiological enjoyment of your body and the body of others.

- *Sexualization*- The use of sexuality to control others.

- *Intimacy*- Emotional closeness to another person.

- *Sexual health and reproduction*- Attitudes and behaviors related to producing children, care of sex and reproductive organs and health consequences of sexual behavior.

- *Sexual identity*- The developed sense of who you are sexually including sense of maleness and femaleness.

Adapted from:Life Planning Education. (1995). Advocates for Youth. Washington, DC

Session Five

Decision-Making

Goal: To introduce decision-making.

Objectives:

1. Increase participant's knowledge of the importance of good decision-making.
2. Participants will verbalize the riskiest decisions an adolescent might make.

Methods:

Conduct an interactive activity to introduce decision-making.

Procedure:

1. Number four small bags one through four and put the following objects in the corresponding bags:
   - ✓ **Bag 1:banana and condom**
   - ✓ **Bag 2:water-filled soda bottle**
   - ✓ **Bag 3:onion**
   - ✓ **Bag 4:dollar bill and IOU for $1**
   - ✓ **Fold the bags and staple at the top.**

2. Ask the group for examples of decisions they have made today:
   - ✓ **What to wear?**
   - ✓ **What to have for breakfast?**
   - ✓ **What time to get up?**

3. Emphasis that everyone must make small, relatively unimportant decisions on a daily basis. With big and important issues, it is helpful to know how to make good decisions.

4. Ask three volunteers to pick a bag. Tell the remaining group members to try and influence the volunteers of which bag to pick, and give the volunteers the option of using the group's advice.

5. Ask the volunteers why they chose the bag. Emphasize to the group that the volunteers had no information about what was in the bag and without information, it is hard to make an informed decision.

6. Give the volunteers the opportunity to examine the bags by feeling or manipulating the bags, **but not opening them.** They will also be allowed to exchange their first choice for the remaining fourth bag, or exchange among each volunteer.

7. **Have the volunteers open their bags and display the contents. They should then offer to the group why they chose their particular bag; what information did they rely on.**

Discussion points:
1. What are some key factors needed in decision-making? (i.e. information, time, consequences)
2. How did you feel when you were being pressured by the group?
3. What things/factors influence decision-making for you? (i.e. media, friends, culture, parents)
4. What are some risky decisions an adolescent can make?

Goal: To develop a model for effective decision-making.
Objectives:
1. To increase participants ability to make good decisions.
2. To practice good decision-making.

Methods: Interactive activity will introduce the Three C's to Good Decision-Making
Procedure:
Part 1:
1. Using newsprint, create a poster-sized model of the Three C's to Good Decision-Making.
2. Distribute handout "Three C's to Good Decision-Making" handout..
3. Emphasize to the group that the decisions made in the previous activity were not serious ones and had **no significant consequences.**
4. Distribute index cards and ask participants to record one serious decision that they are currently facing, and one serious decision they know a friend to be facing. Assure them that all responses *will be kept confidential.*
5. Collect cards, record responses on newsprint, and file cards.
6. Using the poster-sized model of the Three C's to Good Decision-Making, ask for and record responses to each of the components:
   a. **Challenges**
   b. **Choices**
   c. **Consequences (positive and negative)**

7. Ask the group to record a summary of how what is on the board could help you make a good decision.
8. Ask the group to record the responses to the following questions:
   a. What certain consequences warn you immediately to make another choice?
   b. When facing a decision, how could you find other choices?

35

      c.   How can you explore all the possible consequences (positive and negative) of a particular choice?

Part 2:

Interactive activity: Practice good decision-making using the decisions recorded on index cards earlier.

Procedure:

1. Randomly select two decisions from the file.
2. Randomly select two decisions from the file.
3. Have the group construct their model of the Three C's.
4. Use this model to determine what choices led to each decision.

Discussion Points:

1. What makes decision-making difficult?
2. Can you apply this model to a decision you or a friend is currently facing?
3. What decisions have you made in the past that affected other people?

Adapted from: Advocates for Youth. (1995) <u>Life Planning Education.</u> Washington, DC

Three C'S To Good Decision Making

Challenge (or decision) you are facing:

_____

_____

_____

Choices you have:

     Choice 1   _____

     Choice 2   _____

     Choice 3   _____

Consequences of each choice:

     Positive   Negative

     Choice 1   _____

     Choice 2   _____

     Choice 3   _____

Your decision is: _____

Your reason (s)? _____

Adapted from: Advocates for Youth. (1995) Life Planning Education. Washington, DC

Session Six

Reducing Pregnancy Risk

Goal: Assess the current knowledge level of participants about reducing sexual risks.

Objective: Participants will be pre-tested and post-tested to determine knowledge of factors related to sexual risks.

Methods:
1. Administer Pre and Post-Test
2. Discuss questions and responses.

Discussion Points:
1. The only sure way of avoiding pregnancy is to abstain.
2. Some forms of contraception are more effective than others.

Goal: To encourage abstinence from sexual intercourse.

Objective: Increase participant's knowledge of the benefits abstinence.

Method: Lecture

Emphasis will be placed on abstinence as being the only form of contraception that is 100 percent effective. It is the choice of many people, especially young unmarried people. Many people share this preference because they want to avoid pregnancy and sexually transmitted diseases. Some choose this method because they desire to act consistently with their religious beliefs. Abstinence can be a test of the endurance of love beyond sexual attraction.

Some people have already made the choice to have sex. They may feel good about it, or they may feel uncomfortable about it. Even a person who has already had sex, once or many times, can choose to say "NO" now. The choice belongs to the individual.

Goal: Review strategies that assess one's readiness for sexual intercourse.

Objective: Increase participant's self-awareness of readiness for sexual activity.

Methods:
1. Self-assessment and group discussion.
   a. Administer self-assessment "AM I READY FOR SEX?"
   b. Emphasize to the group that their responses will remain confidential and that even though some of the questions may not apply to their current situation, this assessment should be reviewed later when the decision is at hand.
2. Close activity with the following discussion points:

Discussion Points:
1. The way you answer these questions should alert you to areas of your present relationship that may need attention before you consider or continue sexual intimacy.
2. Your willingness and ability to answer these questions for yourself and discuss with your partner shows maturity.
3. Mature people know that sexual intercourse is too important to just let IT HAPPEN.
4. Sex drive can lead people into serious trouble unless they control it through willpower and make conscious decisions about intercourse.

Goal: To demonstrate the risk of pregnancy during intercourse with and without contraception.

Objective: Increase participants' awareness of the risk of pregnancy during intercourse both with and without contraception.

Materials:
- **105** small wrapped candies of one color and **95** of a second color (butterscotch, peppermints, hard candies); two paper bags; copies of the handout and poster size of "Contraceptive Failure Rates;" newsprint and markers.

Methods: Group activity/demonstration.
1. Put 90 candies of one color and 10 candies of the other color in a paper bag marked "Intercourse *without* Contraception." The 90 candies represent unplanned pregnancy.
2. Put 85 candies of the second color and 15 of the first color in the remaining bag marked "Intercourse *with* Contraception". The 15 candies of the first color will represent unplanned pregnancy.
   a. Emphasize to the group that people often do not understand the high risk of pregnancy associated with sexual intercourse without contraception.
   b. Inform the group that the focus of this activity will be pregnancy risk without contraception. Ask the group to imagine 100 heterosexual couples who are having sex regularly for one year. How many of those couples would they predict would be pregnant by the end of the year without the use of contraception? Responses will be recorded on newsprint.
3. Display the bag "Intercourse without Contraception." And explain that the candies in the bag represent the exact percentage of pregnancy that is risked by unprotected intercourse.

39

4. Show the group which candies represent "pregnancy" and which represents "no pregnancy." Ask each participant to draw a candy form the bag, without looking, and hold it up. If the candy represents "pregnancy," that means one of the 100 imaginary couples having sex without contraception has gotten pregnant.

5. When everyone has drawn, ask how many drew a candy representing unplanned pregnancy. Emphasize that 85 out of 100 couples having sex without contraception for one year would get pregnant.

6. Now ask the group to predict how many couples having sexual intercourse with the use of contraception for one year would get pregnant. Record responses on the newsprint.

7. Repeat the process with the bag of candies representing "Intercourse with Contraception." Ask each participant to draw a candy form the bag, without looking, and hold it up. Ask how may drew an unplanned pregnancy this time. Emphasize that contraception does make a difference. Only 15 out of 100 couples who have sex for a year get pregnant if they use contraception.

8. Display the poster of contraceptive failure rate and ask someone to explain how to read it. Be sure teens interpret the chart correctly. (For example, out of 100 women using the pill for contraception, only three to five will become pregnant by the end of a year.)

Evaluation/discussion?

1. What was the most important thing you learned from this activity?

2. How did you feel when you drew candy from the "without contraception" bag? How about the "with contraception" bag?

3. When pregnancy occurs, there is also a risk of infection with HIV and/or another STD.

4. If you were pregnant, how would contracting an STD affect your pregnancy?

5. What fact would you share with friends who are engaging in sexual intercourse?

EAT THE CANDY
Adapted from: Barth, R. (1993). Reducing the risk: Building skills to prevent pregnancy STD & HIV. Santa Cruz, CA: ETR Associates.

Reducing Risk of Pregnancy Pre-Test

1. What is abstinence?
2. What is contraception?
3. Describe or define the following terms:
   a. Norplant
   b. Oral contraceptives
   c. Intrauterine Device
   d. Male condom
   e. Female condom
   f. Diaphragm and spermicidal jelly
   g. Withdrawal (pulling out)
   h. Cervical cap
   i. Natural Family Planning (rhythm method)
   j. Foam, jelly cream or vaginal contraceptive film
4. List three contraceptive methods
5. What is the most effective method of contraception?

Adapted from: Source: Advocates for Youth. (1995) Life Planning Education. Washington, DC:

41

Reducing Risk of Pregnancy Post Test

1. Is abstinence a form of contraception?
2. What is contraception?
3. Rank the top three forms of contraception based on their effectiveness.
   a. Norplant
   b. Oral contraceptives
   c. Intrauterine Device
   d. Male condom
   e. Female condom
   f. Diaphragm and spermicidal jelly
   g. Withdrawal (pulling out)
   h. Cervical cap
   i. Natural Family Planning (rhythm method)
   j. Foam, jelly cream or vaginal contraceptive film
4. What is the most effective method of contraception?

Adapted from: Source: Advocates for Youth. (1995) Life Planning Education. Washington, DC:

SELF-ASSESSMENT
Am I Ready For Sex?

- What place does this relationship have in my life?
- What qualities do I want in my partner?
- Does my current partner have these qualities?
- Do I trust my partner?
- Where are the pressures to have sex coming from? Is it my own biological desire or is it that "everyone else is 'DOING IT'"?
- What does/will sexual intercourse mean for me?
- What are the benefits of remaining abstinent?
- How does having sexual intercourse relate to my own personal values and religious beliefs?
- Does the person make me feel loved in non-sexual ways? Love should be expressed in doing favors, hugs, trust, gift giving, honesty, kissing and being sensitive to each other's moods.
- Have we both agreed on the best way to prevent pregnancy, and on the use of condoms to prevent sexually transmitted diseases?

Source: Turner, L., Sizer, F., Whitney, E., & Wilks, B. (1988) Life Choices: Health concepts and strategies. West Publishing Company: New York.

Goal Setting

Goal: To assist participants with the development of skills needed to form healthy and realistic life goals.

Objectives: Participants will:

1. Discuss the process of assessing and planning for the future.
2. Following guidelines for goal setting, participants will choose goals for themselves and construct plans for achieving those goals.
3. Affirm that without thoughtful planning they are risking their futures.

Methods:

1. Lecture and Group Discussion:
    a. Explain to the group that all the discussions and activities prior to this point have been intended to help provide knowledge and skills needed to successfully transition into young adulthood.
    b. Realizing and comprehending that you have a future may be difficult. This program was designed to help you appreciate and understand yourselves and to help you "be all you can be."
    c. Reflecting back on the benefits of positive attitudes, participants will be encouraged to remain enthusiastic and confident about envisioning a positive future possible through **their own efforts.**
    d. Participants will be assured that it is not necessary that they know exactly what they want to be or do within the next five to ten years, but it is necessary to be aware of their own personal future and at a minimum, be able to generalize or prepare for it. Emphasize to the group that the future begins now.
2. Group Activity
    a. Distribute the handout "Where Am I Going?"
        1. Read each statement and ask participants what each means to them.
    b. Distribute "Guidelines for Goal Setting."
        1. Read and discuss.
    c. Explain to the group that this activity will:
        1. Help them identify a personal goal they have.
        2. Help them identify the personal rewards they will receive upon reaching that goal.

3. Help them identify the barriers that may deter them from reaching the goal.
4. Help them identify what they could do to work through the barriers.

d. The group will be encouraged to continue to work toward their goals.

Source: Advocates for Youth. (1995) <u>Life Planning Education.</u> Washington, DC:

Where Am I Going?

Become aware of yourself: You must become aware of your physical, mental and emotional self. Be aware of your unconscious drives and motivations.

Ask yourself: What am I doing? Am I getting what I want or what I need?

Take responsibility for your situation: This means that you must be willing to accept responsibility for the results of your behavior.

Look at the possible alternatives: What other choices of behavior are open to you?

What choices are more consistent with your values?

Choose among the alternative choices: What general things do you really want to work on? What specific behaviors do you want to try for the next week or month?

Affirm your decision: Imagine yourself practicing this new behavior in a variety of situations. Place a poster of a motto reinforcing your chosen quality or behavior in a permanent place where you will see it often.

Develop a plan of action: Map out in detail the specific steps of your plan in the order you will need to take them.

ACT NOW! Evaluate the outcome: Evaluate the results of your attempt. What happened? How did you feel during and afterwards? If you are willing to add this new behavior or attitude to your self-inventory, you have **GROWN.**

Adpated from:Core-Gebhart, P., Hart,, S. & Young, M. (1994) Sex Can Wait: An abstinence based sexuality education curriculum for middle school. ETR Associates: Santa Cruz

Guidelines For Goal Setting

Conceivable: You must be able to conceptualize the goal so that it is understandable and be able to clearly identify the first step or two.

Believable: In addition to being consistent with your personal value system, you must believe you can reach the goal. Believing you can achieve your goals goes back to the need to have a positive, affirmative feeling about yourself.

Achievable: The goals you set must be accomplishable with your given strengths and abilities. For example, if you were an overweight 45-year-old, it would be foolish for you to set the goal of running the four-minute mile in the next three months that would not be an achievable goal.

Controllable: If your goals include the involvement of another person, you should first obtain his or her permission, or state your goal as an invitation. For example, if your goal is to take someone you like to a movie on Saturday night, the goal will not be acceptable as stated because the person might turn you down. However if you state your goal as merely to invite this person to the movie, it is an acceptable goal.

Measurable: Your goal must be stated so that it is measurable in time and quantity. For example, suppose your goal is to work on your term paper this week. You should specify your goal by saying, "I am going to write 20 pages by three o'clock next Monday afternoon." This way, the goal can be measured, and when Monday comes, you'll know whether or not you have achieved it.

Desirable: Your goal should be something you really want to do, rather than something you feel you should do. There are many things in life that people must do. But highly motivated people must commit a substantial percentage of time to doing things they truly want to do. In other words, while there will always be "musts", what we "want" is vital to changing styles of being and living.

Stated with no alternative: You should set one goal at a time. Research has shown that people who say they want to do one thing or another, giving themselves an alternative, seldom get beyond the "or". They do neither. This does not imply inflexibility. Flexibility in action implies an ability to make a judgment that some action you are involved in is inappropriate, unnecessary or the result of a bad decision. Even though you may begin with one goal, you can stop at any time and replace it with a new one. Upon changing, you must again state your goal without an alternative.

Growth facilitating: Your goal should never be destructive to yourself, others or to society. Instead, it should foster growth.

Source: Core-Gebhart, P., Hart,, S. & Young, M. (1994) Sex Can Wait: An abstinence based sexuality education curriculum for middle school. ETR Associates: Santa Cruz

Session Eight

West African Dance and Rhythms

Goal: To increase participants' awareness of the various roles of traditional West African dance and rhythms.

Objectives: Upon completion, participants will be able to:
1. Define traditional dance.
2. List several traditional West African dances and their functions.

Methods:
1. Lecture
   a. Traditional dance is defined as dance that is passed on through generations. Traditional dance often imitates daily life or animals or has ritual and/or tribal aspects. African dance cannot and should not be separated from music, specifically the drum. Music in the form of song, hand clapping or some form of percussion is always present with African dance. The relationship between the African dancer and drummer suggests being linked or married, both assuming an important role throughout the particular event, which has caused them to come together. The dancer controls the tempo of the drum and the drum controls elements of change in the dance.
   b. Our African ancestors came to America with cultural traditions that have been maintained and passed on from generation to generation through storytelling, song and dance and caused for a permanent link to be made between Africa and America.
   c. In West Africa, dance has a functional role and is included in every activity between birth and death. There are dances for secret societies, healings, weddings, funerals, naming ceremonies, harvest, wars, passing from childhood into adulthood, welcoming of visitors and the coronation of a new chief or king. For each of life's activities there is a ceremony or rite of passage, whose purpose is to assist the individual in passing from one position to another. In the Sokoto State of Nigeria, the Birnin Kebbi people survive by fishing and farming. Therefore, many of their native dances reflect these daily activities. Lenjengo is a dance of Senegal and Gambia which imitates the movements of a bird that lives in the Casamance area of this region. The AkanKan dance addresses the harvest of grains in

the Casamance region. Its movements depict gathering the grain from the fields, cleaning it and finally celebrating the successful harvest.

Goal: Prepare program participants for a dance/rhythm presentation to be performed at the Celebration Ceremony.
Objective: Participants will be able to present a nine minute choreographed traditional dance.
Methods: Dance & Rhythm Classes
1. Imani Edu-Tainers African Dance Company will conduct African dance and rhythms classes. Dance and rhythm instruction will be offered weekly. To prepare for the Celebration Ceremony, the participants will primarily focus on learning dances and rhythms that celebrate initiation and rites of passage.

Resources: Asante, K.W., (Ed). (1996). African dance: An artistic, historical and philosophical inquiry. Trenton, New Jersey: African World Press, Inc.

Delaney, C. H. (1995). Rites of passage in adolescence. Adolescence, 30. (120), 892-897.

Thompson, I. (1993). Traditional African dance: An excellent approach to fitness and health. (ERIC No. Ed379240). New York.

BIBLIOGRAPHY

ADAMS, P. (2005). ADOLESCENT AND PEDIATRIC GYNECOLOGY — US ADOLESCENT Pregnancy Rates: Declining, But More Progress is Needed. Current Opinion in Obstetrics & Gynecology, 17 (5), 453.

Advocates For Youth. (2002) Adolescent sexual behavior: Demographics. Washington, DC: Author.

Advocates for Youth. (2002) Guide to Implementing TAP: A Peer Education Program to Prevent HIV and STI (2nd edition), Washington, DC

Advocates For Youth. (2009) Parent-child communication: Promoting healthy youth. Washington, DC: Author.

African Ancestored Database. (1997). http://members. aol.com.afriamgene/ surnames/sig-names.html

Ansa K. (1993). Adinkrah Symbols. http://auvsi.org/kemet/adinkra.htm.

Asante, M.K. (1987). The Afrocentric idea. Philadelphia: Temple Press.

Asante, K.W., (Ed). (1996). African dance: An artistic, historical and philosophical inquiry. Trenton, New Jersey: African World Press, Inc.

Barone, C., Isokovics, J., Ayers, T., Datz, S., & Voyce, C. (1996). High-risk sexual behavior among young urban students. Family Planning Perspectives, 28. 69-74.

Barth, R. (1993). Reducing the risk: Building skills to prevent pregnancy STD & HIV. Santa Cruz, CA: ETR Associates.

Belgrave, F.Z., Van Oss Marin, B., & Chambers, D.B. (2000). Culture, contextual, and interpersonal predictors of risky sexual attitudes among urban African American girls in early adolescence. Culture Diversity and Ethnic Minority Psychology, 6 (3), 309-322.

Black Americans of Achievement. (1993). BAOA, Inc., San Diego, CA.

Brookins, C. (1996). Promoting ethnic identity development in African-American youth: The role of rites of passage. Journal of Black Psychology, 22. (3), 388-417.

Butler, E. & Glennen, R. (1991). Initiations rituals: Sanctioning rites of passage rituals to increase involvement. ED365903.

Card, J., Niego, S., Mallari, A., & Farrell, W. (1996). Program archive on sexuality health and adolescence: Promising "prevention programs in a box." Family Planning Perspectives, 28. 210-220.

Catalano, R., Berglund, M.L., Ryan, J., Lonczak, H., Hawkins, D. (2002). Positive Youth Development in the United States: Research Findings on Evaluations of Positive youth Development Programs. Prevention & Treatment. 5 (15), 1-111.

Children's Aid Society. (1994). Teen pregnancy prevention program. New York. Author.

Coley, R., & Chase-Lansdale, L. (1998). Adolescent Pregnancy and Parenthood: Recent Evidence and Future Directions. American Psychologist. 53 (20), 152-166.

Community Needs Report. (1995). Prevention of teen pregnancy. Pennsylvania. United Way of Lancaster County.

Core-Gebhart, P., Hart,, S. & Young, M. (1994) Sex Can Wait: An abstinence based sexuality education curriculum for middle school. ETR Associates: Santa Cruz

Davis, L. (1996). Components of promising teen pregnancy prevention programs. Advocates for Youth National Pregnancy Prevention Clearinghouse.

Delaney, C. H. (1995). Rites of passage in adolescence. Adolescence, 30. (120), 892-897.

Delaney, G., (1998, September 4). Minority population on the rise. Intelligencer Journal, 69, pp. A1, A7.

Dixon, A., Schoonmaker, C. Philliber, W. (2000). Adolescence, 35. (139), 425-429).

Flannery, D., Torquanti, J. & Lindemeier, L. (1994). The method and meaning of emotional expression and experience during adolescence. Journal of Adolescent Research, 9. 8-27.

Foster, H., Greene, L., & Smith, M. (1990). A model for increasing access: Teenage pregnancy prevention. Journal of Health Care For The Poor and Underserved, 1. 136-146.

Frost, J.J., & Forrest, J.D. (1995). Understanding the impact of effective teenage pregnancy preventions programs. Family Planning Perspectives, 27. 188-195.

Galbraith, J., Ricardo, I., Stanton, B., Black, M., Feigelman, S., Kaljee, L. (1996). Health Education Quarterly, 23. (3). 383.

Goggins II, L. (1996). African-centered rites of passage and education. Chicago: African American Images.

Heinegg, P. (1997). Free African Americans of North Carolina and Virginia. Baltimore, MD: The Genealogical Publishing Company.

Herdman, C. (1996). Promising adolescent pregnancy prevention programs. Advocates for Youth National Pregnancy Prevention Clearinghouse.

Hill, Jr., P. (2002). Passages: Birth, Initiation, Marriage and Death. http://www.ritesofpassage.org

Hill, Jr., P. (1992). Coming of age: African American male rites of passage. Chicago: African American Images.

Hunter-Geboy, Carol. Life Planning Education: A Youth Development Program. Washington, DC: Advocates for Youth, 1995.

Imani Edu-Tainers African Dance Company. (2011). Mate Masie: Rites of Passage. http://www.imaniafricandance.org

Iverem, E. (1988). Rites of passage. Essence, 19. (8).

Jemmott, J.B., Jemmott, L.S. Fong, G. T. (1992). Reductions in HIV Risk-Associated Sexual Behaviors Among Black Male Adolescents: Effects of an AIDS Prevention Intervention. American Journal of Public Health. 82. 372-377.

Kepple, D. (1998). Tracing Your History. Dayton Daily News. Dayton, Ohio. http://members.aol.com.gfsclint/bennie1.html

Kirby, D. (1997). No easy answers: Research findings on programs to reduce teen pregnancy. A research review commissioned by The National Campaign to Prevent Teen Pregnancy Task Force on Effective Programs and Research.

Kojo, G. (1998). Akan Cultural Symbols Project. http://marshall.edu/akanartintro.html

Lancaster County Health Partnership. (1997). Lancaster County Health Profile.

Life Planning Education. (1995). Advocates for Youth. Washington, DC

Madhubuti, H.R., & Madhubuti, S.L. (1994). African-Centered Education: Its Value, Importance, and Necessity in the development of black children. Chicago: Third World Press. Mann-McFarlane, S. (1998). Akuaba: Rites of passage to prevent adolescent pregnancy. http://www.geocities.com/hotsptings/villa/5453

Maynard, R.A. (1997). Kids having kids: Economic costs and social consequences of teen pregnancy. Washington, DC: Urban Institute Press.

Miller, B. C., Card, J.J., Paikoff, R.L., & Peterson, J.L. (Eds.). (1992). Preventing adolescent pregnancy. Newbury Park, CA: Sage.

Miller. B.C., & Paikoff, R.L. (1992). Comparing adolescent pregnancy prevention programs: Methods and results. In B.C. Miller, J.J. Card, R.L. Paikoff, & J.L. Peterson (Eds.), Preventing adolescent pregnancy (pp. 265-294). Newbury Park, CA: Sage.

Moore, K. (1996). Facts at a glance, reporting final 1994 and preliminary 1995 data on teen fertility in the United States. Washington, DC: Child Trends, Inc.

Moore, K. & Sugland, B. (1996). Next best bets: Approaches to preventing adolescent childbearing. Washington, DC: Child Trends, Inc.

Moore, K., Miller, B., Glei, D., Morrison, D. (1995). Adolescent sex, contraception and childbearing: A review of recent research. Washington, DC: Child Trends, Inc.

Moore, M., Gilyard, G., & King, K., (1987). Transformation: A rites of passage manual for African American girls. New York, NY: Stars Press.

Mutisya, M. (1996). Demythologization and demystification of African initiation rites: A positive and meaningful educational aspect heading for extinction. Journal of Black Studies, 27. (1), 94-103.

O'Neil, D. (2007). Process of Socialization: Rites of Passage. http://anthro.palomar.edu/social/soc/4.htm

Onwirah, N. (1996). Monday's Girl. The Library of African Cinema. Penn State University.

Ottenberg, S. (1992). The beaded bands of bafodea. African Arts, 25. (2).

Penn, M.L. & Watkins, D. (2008). "Pathognomic Versus Developmentally Appropriateness Self-Focus During Adolescence: Theoretical Concerns and Clinical Implications". Psychotherapy. In Human Development, 3rd Edition. R. Deissner (ED) Publisher. McGraw-Hill. New York: NY.

Pennsylvania Department of Health (1995). Pennsylvania Vital Statistics. http://www.portal.state.pa.us/portal/server.pt?open=514&objID =651925&mode=2

Philliber, S., & Namerow, P. (1995). Trying to maximize the odds: Using what we know to prevent teen pregnancy. Atlanta, GA: Centers for Disease Control and Prevention.

Phinney, J.S. (1992). The Multi-Group Ethnic Identity Measure: A new scale for use with diverse groups. Journal of Adolescent Research, 7(2), 156-176.

Phinney, J.S., & Chavira, V. (1995). Parental ethnic socialization and adolescent coping with problems related to ethnicity. Journal Research Adolescence, 5. 31-53.

Phinney, J.S. & Tarver, S. (1988). Ethnic identity search and commitment in black and white eighth graders. Journal of Adolescence, 8(3), 256-277.

Potts, R. (2003). Emancipatory Education Versus School-Based Prevention in African American Communities. American Journal of Community Psychology. 31, 1 / 2. 173-183.

Santelli, J.S., Lindberg, L.D., Finer, L.B., & Singh, S. (2007). Explaining recent declines in adolescent pregnancy in the United States: the contribution of abstinence an improved contraceptive use. <u>American Journal of Public Health. 1</u>. (150-6).

St. Lawrence, J.S., Brasfield, T.L., Jefferson, K.W., Alleyne, E., O'Bannon, R.E. III. (1995). Comparison of Education Versus Behavioral Skills Training Interventions in Lowering Sexual HIV Risk Behavior of Substance-Dependent Adolescents. <u>Journal of Consulting and Clinical Psychology. 63.</u> (2). 154-157

The African Ancestored Database. (1997). <u>http://members. aol.com.afriamgene/ surnames/sig-names.html</u>

The Afrigeneas Homepage. (1998). <u>http://www.msstate. edu/Archives/History/ afrigen/</u>

The Centers for Disease Control and Prevention. (1995). 1995 Youth Risk Behavior Surveillance System. <u>http://www.cdc.gov</u>

The Centers for Disease Control and Prevention. (1996). National Center for Health Statistics: Pennsylvania Health Facts. <u>http://www.cdc.gov</u>

The Centers for Disease Control and Prevention. (1997). Morbidity and Mortality weekly Report: State Specific Birth Rates for Teenagers - United States, 1990-1996. <u>http://www.cdc.gov/mmwr</u>

The Centers for Disease Control and Prevention. (1997). Monthly Vital Statistics Report. <u>http://cdc.gov</u>

The Centers for Disease Control. (1998). National Center for Health Statistics: Teenage Births in the United States: State Trends, 1991 - 1996, an Update.

The National Campaign to Prevent Teen and Unplanned Pregnancy. (2007) Ten tips for parents to help their children avoid teen pregnancy. Washington, DC: Author.

Thompson, I. (1993). Traditional African dance: An excellent approach to fitness and health. (ERIC No. Ed379240). New York.

Traore, R. (2007). Implementing Afrocentricity: Connecting Students of African Descent to Their Cultural Heritage. <u>The Journal of Pan African Studies. 1</u>. (10), 62-78.

Turner, L., Sizer, F., Whitney, E., & Wilks, B. (1988) Life Choices: Health concepts and strategies. West Publishing Company: New York.

United Nations, (1991). <u>Demographic Yearbook.</u> New York: Author.

Van Gennep, A. (1960). <u>The rites of passage.</u> Chicago: The University of Chicago Press.

Ventura, S., Curtin, S., & Mathews, T. (1997). Teen births in the United States: National and state trends, 1990-1996. <u>National Vital Statistics System.</u> Hyattsville, Maryland: National Center for Health Statistics.

Warfield-Coppock, N. (1992). The rites of passage movement: A resurgence of African-centered practices for socializing African American youth. Journal of Negro Education, 61. (4).

Warfield-Coppock, N., & Harvey, A. (1989). Teen-age pregnancy prevention: A rites of passage resource manual. Washington, DC: MAAT Institute For Human And Organizational Enhancement, Inc.

Watts-Hines, T., Taylor, W. & Chan. W. (2007) African American females adolescents and antecedents of pregnancy. Masters Abstracts International, 46-01. (346)

Well-Tempered Web Designs. (2007) West African Wisdom: Adinkra Symbols & Meanings. http://adinkra.org/